Safety and Challenge
for Japanese learners
of English

professional
perspectives

Safety and Challenge
for Japanese learners
of English

Peta Gray
Sue Leather

Eᴎɢʟɪꜱʜ Tᴇᴀᴄʜɪɴɢ *professional*

Published by First Person Publishing Limited
15 Baldwyn Gardens, London W3 6HJ
and DELTA Publishing, 39 Alexandra Road,
Addlestone, Surrey KT15 2PQ

First published 1999

ISBN 0 953 30982 7

Designed by David Dutch

Printed in Britain

Acknowledgements

The publisher would like to thank Jonathan Chandler, Julie Dyson,
Roger Hunt, Robin Price and Paul Snowden who all provided useful
comment on the manuscript.

Author acknowledgements

We would like to thank our former colleagues and students at the
Cambridge Academy of English, where *Safety and Challenge* was born.
Special thanks to Mario Rinvolucri, Yumi Shioiri, and all the students
from Tokai Women's College who taught us so much about Japanese
people and culture.

Contents

	Page
Introduction	7

Section A

Building on Existing Strengths and Previous Experience — 11

Section B

Developing New Models of Learning — 17

Section C

Developing Discussion Skills — 23

Section D

Cultural Surf-riding — 29

Section E

Letting Go of Tension — 35

Section F

Taking the Focus off Language — 41

Introduction

The Background

Japanese learners have specific needs which go largely unaddressed by the prevailing methodology in language schools and on college language courses. The western focus on student participation, risk-taking and individuality contrasts sharply with the Japanese educational tradition. In Japan these features do not have the positive values accorded them in the West. This can often lead to misunderstanding, confusion and inadequate learning: the ingredients of culture shock.

In addition, mainstream teacher-training courses in many contexts do not prepare teachers to teach Japanese learners effectively. Nor are teachers helped by published material, most of which does not adequately address the specific conditions of teaching Japanese students.

In particular, most material fails to bridge the culture gap or to address the specific problems that Japanese students encounter in trying to communicate spontaneously in the classroom. Japanese, and to a lesser extent other Asian learners, simply cannot be taught in the same way as students from predominantly western cultures without significant underachievement.

Safety and Challenge addresses these fundamental pedagogical questions and offers what we believe are new answers. We hope that it will be helpful for teachers working in Japan, perhaps preparing students for visits abroad and for teachers of Japanese students throughout the English-speaking world.

The Challenge for the Teacher

What do non-Japanese teachers find challenging about teaching Japanese learners?

In our workshops and seminars in a number of different educational contexts, teachers have come up with various features of Japanese student behaviour, which include:

- long pauses before answering
- lack of eye contact
- long silences
- not initiating
- very quiet voices that are very difficult to hear
- consulting with other members of the group before answering
- insistence on accuracy.

These features can be extremely frustrating for teachers, but only because of the cultural expectations they have of classroom behaviour. The aim of this book is to help the non-Japanese teacher to decode the behaviour of their students in the classroom and to understand the different cultural and educational expectations which are the ingredients of the encounter. So, for example, whilst in the West we put a high cultural value on standing out from the crowd and saying 'I think...', this is not so in Japan, where it is more likely to be seen as immodest, even selfish. With this information, we can more readily understand why Japanese students consult with other members of the group before answering.

Our aim is to 'unlock' the undoubted joys of teaching Japanese learners, who bring with them to the classroom strengths which we are sometimes in danger of undervaluing. These strengths include a very high awareness of the needs of their companions as individuals, great discipline and a wonderful aptitude for teamwork.

Much is said about confidence when talking about Japanese learners. They 'lack confidence' about their ability to speak about themselves. This is certainly true and this book deals with that area quite comprehensively. However, we also feel that teachers often lack confidence when dealing with their Japanese students. They feel that they don't know enough about Japanese culture: they are afraid of offending students' sensibilities and feel wary of the silence. In talking about the Japanese there is often a tendency to exoticisation and mystification which can only make us less effective as teachers. Our intention here is to de-exoticise, to de-mystify. The rationale for each activity very often contains information on cultural background and code words. Our aim here is to give teachers information which will help to explain some cross-cultural misunderstandings which have a bearing on what happens in the classroom.

Safety and Challenge

Safety and Challenge is aimed at teachers of Japanese students in a number of different contexts. Some of the activities are intended for use with students in a monolingual setting, others for the multilingual classroom; most are for use in either. It is important that the activities are not merely a series of 'one-offs', but are seen by the teacher as part of a consistent and integrated approach to Japanese learners. We have therefore included a rationale for each activity and also links, alternatives and development ideas. However, the busy teacher who needs a useable activity quickly will certainly be able to use the activities as they are.

The aim of *Safety and Challenge* then is not only to provide the teacher with a number of activities that work well in the classroom, but also to provide a consistent philosophy for teaching Japanese students in monolingual and multilingual classes. The underlying construct is that of the opposing yet complementary concepts of *safety* and *challenge*.

It is our contention that, while these conditions may be a prerequisite of all learning, they have a particularly important role to play in the teaching of Japanese students.

By *safety* we mean a learning context in which the students will feel that nothing too 'frightening' will happen to them, that they will not be pushed into making fools of themselves, of losing face. The concept of face *(kao)* is extremely important in Japanese culture and teachers need to be aware of its power and resonance.

Safety can be achieved for Japanese learners in the classroom by focusing on activities which come naturally to them because of cultural factors and their previous educational experience. So, particularly at the beginning, there will be a focus on team activities rather than individual ones. The team spirit *(batsu)* is a great source of support for Japanese students in a new environment or in any new and challenging situation. Activities which have a high level of safety, then will not put individuals 'on the spot'. They will allow students to practise, perhaps in pairs, before they have to perform. They will also perhaps include writing and silent activities such as *Silent Discussion* in Section C. Activities in Section A - *Building on Existing Strengths and Previous Experience* also have a high level of safety.

By *challenge* we mean high-risk activities which may be counter-cultural and therefore more difficult. What do Japanese students find most difficult? Spontaneous speech, listening for general rather than specific meaning, activities in which the individual is more exposed, perhaps having to perform on his/her own. Activities which take the students' attention away from accuracy and towards fluency and communication will also be challenging. High challenge activities will be found in Section D *Cultural Surf-riding*.

However, though we present the two concepts of *safety* and *challenge* as discrete entities, we believe that both should be present in all classroom activities. Challenging activities will not be successful, particularly with Japanese learners, unless there is a context of safety. Our most challenging counter-cultural activities are always done within a framework of safety. The concepts are not polar opposites, therefore, but complementary. We represent this visually in all the activities, so that you can see at a glance the balance between *safety* and *challenge*. In our visual representation, shown below, *safety* is the outer ring, always 'holding' the *challenge*, which is smaller or bigger depending on the nature of the activity.

- high safety
- safety and challenge equally balanced
- high challenge

It is, then, primarily the interplay between safety and challenge at any given time which makes teaching Japanese learners successful or not. This ultimately comes down to the skill and intuition of the individual teacher in the classroom. This book is intended to help teachers to learn more about their Japanese students, to test the boundaries of *safety* and *challenge* and to develop their teaching skills. As such we hope that it will not just be seen as a series of successful activities, but as a real contribution to our understanding of how Japanese learners operate and learn in the classroom, and how as teachers we can facilitate that process.

The Activities

The materials are divided into six sections. *Building on Existing Strengths and Previous Experience* starts from where the Japanese learner is 'coming from' in terms of educational background. The activities here are designed to give the students confidence in what they know already and also in what they have been prepared for by their educational system.

Developing New Models of Learning contains introductory activities to the new ways of behaviour we expect from them in the classroom: focusing less on accuracy, more on fluency; being less concerned about mistakes, picking up language outside the classroom as well as inside.

Developing Discussion Skills aims to introduce learners to the very different way in which we have discussions in our culture and in our classrooms. The activities are a mixture of high safety and high challenge.

Cultural Surf-riding is a real 'high challenge' section with very counter-cultural activities. *Letting Go of Tension* is central to what we need to help our Japanese learners to do in the classroom, as is *Taking the Focus off Language*. Sometimes we need to take the focus off language to allow real language work to happen.

The Feeders

There are times when we suggest exercises which go against the received wisdom of the communicative approach in which we have both been trained – exercises such as translation and allowing students to speak in their mother tongue in the classroom. We support these activities wholeheartedly, just as we condemn statements such as 'You should never...'or 'You should always...'.

Our work has been influenced by our training and experience in ELT as well as a number of feeder fields. Peta has a background in drama and co-counselling and has experience of art therapy; Sue has a background in Japanese martial arts training (karate) and co-counselling. We have found these feeder fields to be of great use to us in thinking about our Japanese learners.

A Word on Culture

Are we as teachers of English, teaching language or culture? Are we teaching both? Clearly, this introduction and the activities that follow may provoke these difficult and interesting questions. Some people might put it in an even more challenging way: do we have the right to impose our cultural values on people from another culture? Are we trying to change our students, so that they become more like us?

Our answer is unequivocally 'no', we are not trying to change our Japanese students or to suggest that one way of behaving is better than another. It is a matter of appropriacy, of behaving in a certain context to achieve certain ends. Learning to communicate in a foreign language, in a foreign culture, is so much more than the words which come out of our mouths. There is also body language, voice tone and audibility, eye contact and so many other paralinguistic features. If you have had the experience of learning a language which is very different to your own and of living in a different culture, you know that being linguistically accurate is probably the least of your worries. Cultural inappropriacy is far more likely to cause misunderstanding than using the wrong preposition.

For Japanese students to succeed in certain cultural and educational contexts it is necessary for them to be heard, to speak out, to understand our culture. This does not mean that they will change for ever or become 'western' in their behaviour. It simply means that they will become involved in an educational process, a journey into another culture and that they will be better equipped to feel comfortable there and ultimately to succeed. We are not asking the student to be the only one who tries to understand the foreign culture. It is equally important for teachers to undertake a similar journey in the opposite direction. Journeys into very different cultures are challenging and difficult, but always worthwhile. Do your best, or as the Japanese would say: *Gambatte!*

Peta Gray
Sue Leather

Building on Existing Strengths and Previous Experience

Introduction

The idea behind this section is to exploit fully the undoubted knowledge of English and social strengths that Japanese learners bring with them to the English language-learning classroom. Modern Japanese has quite a number of loanwords from English, for example, which give Japanese learners a ready-made vocabulary. Strategies such as memorisation and rote learning, which the Japanese educational tradition encourages, can also be exploited to good effect, as well as their aptitude for group or teamwork.

Loanwords

Rationale

Japanese is full of very common loanwords from English. The pronunciation of these words has been 'Japanised' so that it is often difficult for us to recognise them. Alongside the description of the activity is a list of loanwords you might like to use for this exercise.

This is a good, confidence-raising activity for a group of low-level learners, who have just arrived from Japan. It is very simple but effective. You can give them an 'instant vocabulary' by just activating these words and getting them to apply the rules of English, not Japanese pronunciation. It makes use of one of the strengths of the Japanese – their ability to work well in teams.

Activity

Class type: monolingual

Level: beginner-intermediate

Materials needed: a list of loanwords – one is provided here, lots of board pens

Preparation time: minimal

Safety/challenge: (•)

Time: 30-45 minutes

Skills: speaking, writing

Procedure

1. Tell the class that they know a lot of words in English already.

2. Elicit an example or two and write them on the board.

3. Put the class into teams of four or five for a competition. Give them a time limit, say five minutes, to write down as many Japanese words with roots in English as they can think of.

4. Divide the board into four.

5. When the time is up, get a representative from each group to come to the board and write up their words. They should all come to the board at the same time and write only their group's words. The winners are the team with most words.

The next stage to this is to get the students to 'translate' their words into English pronunciation. Again, you can do this as a competition. They will almost certainly need help to do it. You can follow it up with some pronunciation work from a pre-recorded wordlist.

Wordlist

kamera (camera)

supotsu-ka (sports car)

erebeta (Am. E elevator, Br. E. lift)

esukareta (escalator)

otobai (motorbike)

shatsu, waishatsu (shirt)

ji-pan (jeans – from 'jean-pants')

epuron (apron)

tepu-rekoda (tape-recorder)

terebi (TV)

rajio (radio)

maiku (microphone, mike)

sutereo (stereo)

beddo (bed – a western bed, not a futon)

kohi (coffee)

sandoitchi (sandwich)

bifuteki (steak)

meron (melon)

orenji (orange)

naifu (knife)

janbo-jetto (jumbo jet)

purezento (present)

depato (department store)

apato (apartment)

boifurendo (boyfriend)

garufurendo (girlfriend)

NB *kohi* is from Dutch and *bifuteki* is from French, but they are sufficiently close to English to work in this context.

Development

A possible follow-up to this for higher levels is to get the students to suggest Japanese words which should be incorporated into English. A possible way of introducing this is with the phrase, 'I can't find an English word or phrase which expresses x'. Again, this can be done as a competition in teams, with the students having to convince you to 'borrow' the words. The idea for this development exercise comes from *Dictation* by Rinvolucri and Davis.

Wordcloud

Rationale

Many Japanese people have an excellent visual memory and this activity makes great use of it. It is also light and great fun; the activity starts off away from language and then moves into it. This approach is one that can be effective with learners of all nationalities, but particularly with Japanese learners.

Activity

Class type: monolingual or multilingual

Level: any level

Materials needed: white/blackboard

Preparation time: minimal

Safety/challenge: (•)

Time: 40 minutes

Skills: using visual memory, vocabulary extension

Procedure

1. Draw a set of six to eight pictures on a piece of paper. They might be objects from a vocabulary set – furniture, for example.

2. Copy them onto the board. Draw a curvy cloud shape around them. Give students one minute to look at them. Do not give any other instructions.

3. Wipe the pictures off the board, one picture at a time, checking back occasionally by pointing at a space and asking what it was (provide the vocabulary if necessary). Leave the shape of the cloud.

4. Give students paper and ask them to reproduce as many of the images as they can remember. They can do this in pairs or individually. Give them a time limit.

5. Suggest they walk round the room visiting others and looking at each other's papers to see what they have remembered. Tell them that they will be asked to try to reproduce the images.

6. When they are seated again, repeat the exercise using different pictures.

7. Ask if anyone has improved their performance. Tell them you will be doing a similar activity later on, but this time using language instead of images.

(This second stage need not be done immediately.)

8. Write up on the board vocabulary you have elicited, or vocabulary from a previous activity or lesson. This may be single words or phrases. Frame them with a cloud shape as before. Again, make sure you have a record of the shape of the cloud and the positions of the items within it.

9. Ask students: 'Who found it very easy and who found it very difficult?' Divide the class into two, pairing those students who found it hard with those who found it easy, and give them a few minutes to talk (in Japanese if they wish).The task of the one who found it easy, is to examine their strategy and describe it to their partner, who should make mental or written notes of what they have been told. You could also ask for volunteers who found they enjoyed the exercise to form a panel to answer questions from the rest of the group. Seat them together, facing the class. (Some students feel safer sitting together in the circle with the rest of the group.)

10. Make a list of the different strategies people employed in the task. This can be made into a large, colourful poster for the wall as a visual reminder of the lesson and as the basis for subsequent lessons (see Development). Make notes for future reference. It can help to know, for example, that Shoko has an outstandingly good visual memory (as a high proportion of Japanese seem to) if she is struggling to understand something one day.

Development

Once you have introduced this activity 'frame' you can use it later:

- to introduce topics or language areas
- to recycle language
- as a warmer
- as a filler.

Dictate/Translate

Rationale

Dictation and translation are both types of exercise that Japanese students will be familiar with. Translation is an exercise that is not often used in the modern ELT classroom. However, at certain times it may be useful to get learners to reflect on the linguistic differences between their mother tongue and English. It also allows the students to show the teacher something!

Safety and Challenge

Activity

Class type: monolingual

Level: any level

Materials needed: slips of paper

Preparation: choose a sentence

Safety/challenge: (•)

Time: 30 minutes

Skills: listening, writing, translating

Procedure

1. Choose a longish sentence, perhaps one that the students are familiar with already from a story or dialogue you've done in class. You can also try using a strongly evocative sentence, for example about Japan or some aspect of Japanese culture. If you haven't got one to hand, a nice one is: 'She had never been to Japan, but people said it was beautiful and she really wanted to go'.

2. Dictate it to them in the usual way.

3. Students check in pairs.

4. Write the sentence on the board and correct their version if necessary.

5. Ask the students to translate the sentence into Japanese. They can work in pairs. Give them a time limit of five minutes.

6. When they've come up with a version, they write it clearly on a slip of paper and hand it in.

7. Lay out all the slips of paper together on a central desk or on the floor.

8. Invite students to come and look at the different versions and check to see whether they are the same.

9. If there are different versions, ask them whether they prefer another one to their own and the reasons why.

10. Ask the authors of a popular version to write it on the board and explain it to you.

Development

A good development from this is to dictate the sentence in English and have the students *immediately* translate it into Japanese. This is a more challenging activity and one which is more likely to bring about a number of different results. The variation in the translated sentences is likely to be greater.

Shadow Puppet Show

Rationale

Rote learning is a strong feature of the Japanese educational system. This activity combines traditional Japanese stories (which students will know well) with rote learning. It is therefore both confidence-giving and very enjoyable. There is a strong tradition of shadow puppets in the East.

Making the puppets can be a very productive activity in terms of language. The students are relaxed and the kind of interactional language you can encourage them to use is very useful e.g. 'Can you pass me the.. ?'Again, the 'taking the focus off language to get at language' approach is very effective.

If you feel that your group would not appreciate making the puppets, you can of course always supply them in the form of clean gloves, socks or cardboard cutouts.

Activity

Class type: monolingual or split multilingual

Level: elementary-advanced

Materials/equipment needed: a bunch of thin cane sticks (you can buy these from gardening shops), paper, scissors, black paint (unless you have black paper), cardboard, OHP

Preparation time: two or three lessons

Safety/challenge: (•)

Skills: speaking, narrative, pronunciation

Procedure

Here is a suggested procedure spanning three lessons. It will of course depend on the length of your lessons and other factors.

First lesson

1. Ask students to form groups of four or five. Each group should choose a traditional Japanese folk tale that they all know well, for example *The Peach Boy*, or *The Repayment of the Crane*.

2. Give them ten minutes' dictionary time to look up keywords and come and write them on the board in a spider diagram around their title.

3. Do some pronunciation work on this vocabulary.

4. Tell the students that they are going to perform this story using shadow puppets.

5. In their groups again, they should write out the skeleton of the story (one person writes).

6. Take these in and correct them.

Second lesson

1. In the same groups students go through the corrected version, adding dialogue to the narrative. So, for example, if the story relates: 'the man refused to go with her any further', students should write a line for the man such as, 'I will not come any further with you. I am tired and my legs will not carry me'.

2. Go round giving help if needed. When each group has completed their narrative they (or you) should photocopy it so that each member of the group has a copy.

3. The group should now decide who is to narrate and who is to be the manipulator and voice of each character. There can be more than one narrator. They can choose someone to be prompt too, if they wish. This person should spend time getting to know the whole text well. Others should learn their parts for homework in preparation for the first rehearsal.

4. In their groups students make the characters of the play by a) drawing a recognisable silhouette painted black, a side view and to an agreed scale, small if you are going to use the OHP as your light source b) mounting it on cardboard cut to shape and c) gluing a stick on it vertically which can be used to hold and manipulate the puppet from below.

5. Put these instructions on the board. Make sure they have the language they will need in this lesson. For example, 'Could you pass me the glue please?' 'Has anyone got the paintbrush?' etc.

Third lesson

1. Once the puppets have been finished, students can start to rehearse their show, taking it in turns to use the OHP. They may wish to add music.

2. When it is polished and everyone knows their parts by heart and can deliver it with clear pronunciation and appropriate stress you could invite another class to be their audience and/or video it for themselves. (There are companies who transfer video recordings onto tape for Japanese systems.)

Development

You can use masks instead of puppets; it's easy to buy them at theatrical and joke shops. If you have students who enjoy making things, you can even make masks out of papier maché or thin card.

It's good fun to encourage students to perform their own stories. You can start this off in a very non-threatening way by telling the students part of a story and asking them to finish it. They then perform the whole story.

Safety and Challenge

Letter to a Character

Rationale

Letter-writing is still very much alive among Japanese people – notice how many letters your Japanese students write and receive! The idea behind this activity is simply to tap into that tradition and to give the students the motivation to write in English.

Activity

Class type: monolingual or multilingual

Level: elementary and above

Materials needed: paper, pens

Preparation: read a story or watch a show

Safety/challenge: (●)

Time: 45 minutes

Skills: writing

Procedure

Choose a reader or story with a strong central character, preferably faced with a dilemma or problem. A lot of readers have this element. You could use for example: *Girl against the Jungle* by Monica Vincent (published by Longman), *Death of a Soldier* by Philip Prowse (published by Heinemann) or *Rebecca* by Daphne du Maurier, retold by Margaret Tarner (published by Heinemann).

This example uses Sue's reader *Desert, Mountain, Sea*, (published by OUP) which we have found to work particularly well with Japanese women learners. The book tells three true stories of 'adventurous women'. There are a number of points in the stories which are suitable for a letter or an email. The procedure would be the same for any reader or story. The main idea is to stop reading at points where the character faces a dilemma, then start a discussion to provoke the writing task.

1. Read the second story, *Climbing Annapurna*, as a class reader. The story is about a team of women who try to reach the summit of Annapurna in the Himalayas. At a number of points the story focuses on the climbing team's leader, Arlene Blum, who has to make a number of difficult decisions which affect other members of the team. Highlight this for the students.

2. As she agonises about her decisions, tell the students that they are her friends and she has asked them for advice. Suggest that they write her an email.

3. Continue reading the story.

4. The climb was successful in that some women reached the summit. However, two women died on the Annapurna expedition. Discuss how Arlene Blum must have felt at the end of the expedition. Did she feel regret about the decisions she made? The students write to her, again as her friend. This activity gives a good focus to a discussion of the story.

Development

This could be used just as a follow-up activity from either watching a show, a film or reading a story. It works well with a dramatic story in which there is a central character with whom the students can identify. An example of a suitable show would be *Miss Saigon*.

Section B

Developing New Models of Learning

Introduction

This section will be particularly useful for teachers who are preparing Japanese learners to study English abroad, or for those helping them to adapt to a different type of classroom in an English-speaking country. Whilst the students' prior educational experience will be of great use to them, there will undoubtedly be new challenges for which they will need support and encouragement. Here, we offer a number of activities intended to train the new skills they will need.

Fishing in the Stream

Rationale

The Japanese educational system values accuracy and certainty. When students listen to native-speaker English – from their landladies, or from the TV or radio – their tendency is to want to understand every single word. This is of course, impossible. Students often become tense and therefore end up understanding less and less.

Listening to normal-speed, authentic, spoken English, is an important aspect of language-learning for a student of any nationality. It helps a learner's vocabulary and knowledge of structure. It is essential for a learner to have a reasonable ability to deal with normal speech in order to be able to operate effectively in society.

Japanese learners are often very aware of their deficiencies when it comes to listening. They know that they have to improve their listening skills if they want to improve their language ability overall.

Here anxiety is removed by not requiring students to make use of their existing knowledge. It's not a test of their language, but of their ears! The idea behind the activity is to get students comfortable with the idea that they can listen to something and not be able to understand words and phrases, and for that to be acceptable. This is counter-cultural and for that reason we call it a high-risk or high challenge activity.

Activity

Class type: best in a monolingual class

Level: any level

Materials needed: a short, authentic listening text – this could be a story read out by the teacher, a listening on tape or video. It should be rapid and natural. With help, it should be within 'listening for general understanding' level of the students.

Preparation time: minimal. Find a suitable listening passage and pick out about five words or short phrases which the students won't know.

Safety/challenge:

Time: 20 minutes

Skills: listening

Procedure

1. Give the students your five words or phrases orally, but without giving their meanings. Five is a good number, as the students have to retain the words in their memory.

2. Play the tape or tell the story. The students simply have to pick out the words or phrases when they hear them. An enjoyable way of doing this is by raising their hands or saying 'hi'.

You can use this as an initial activity in a listening lesson. Continue with a listening for gist exercise, perhaps with true/false questions. It is obviously important that, with your help, the students should get a fair idea of the general meaning. The idea is to build confidence in the idea that they can understand general meaning without understanding every single word.

You may go on to get the students to work out the meaning of the words and phrases from context, though this is not essential.

Development

You may find that, as you do this exercise again and again, the students are able to retain more words. You will also find that you can work with longer listening texts.

Rulesheet

Rationale

The classroom behaviour we expect in western language classrooms often differs greatly from that expected in Japan. In most language classrooms in Japan, for example, learners would not necessarily be expected to participate very actively in lessons. Traditionally, listening to the *sensei* (teacher) is the way that learning takes place. Students are not encouraged to ask questions and certainly not to disagree with the teacher. Japanese society values harmony (*wa*) and the classroom is no exception. This depends on people hiding their feelings and contributing to a surface calm in all situations. Whilst Japan is a dynamic, changing society, students do not normally participate in learning in the way that we expect them to.

Another area likely to cause problems for the Japanese learner is that of making mistakes. Whilst as teachers, we often encourage students to 'just speak', feeling that trying things out is an important aspect of language learning, this is anathema to the Japanese. The importance of *kata*, or form, as shown in the traditional arts, also finds its way into language learning. Students prefer to make sure that an utterance is correct before saying it; making mistakes is not something a Japanese learner does easily.

Japanese learners who find themselves in the kind of language classroom prevalent in English-speaking countries, often have a huge culture shock. Students who are often very successful in their own society, find that the skills they have, are not very useful in the new context. This can obviously be very demotivating. They need to be introduced slowly to the ground rules of their new situation and to have time to adapt.

The idea behind this activity is to open up a dialogue about classroom behaviour with learners and to discuss the differences. It can be used as part of an induction programme for a group of students preparing to go abroad, or for 'new' students once they have arrived. The idea is also for the teacher to learn from listening to his or her students.

NB: We have found this activity very useful with all kinds of groups – students of all nationalities and even with teachers' groups.

Activity

Class type: monolingual or multilingual

Level: elementary-advanced

Materials needed: a list of 'rules' (see below) photocopied for each student.

Preparation time: minimal

Safety/challenge: (●)

Time: 45 minutes

Skills: reading, speaking

Procedure

Prepare a list of classroom rules, some of which could apply, some of which are false or questionable. You could dictate them for further language practice. A possible list could be:

(a) You can call your teacher by his/ her first name.(*)

(b) You can eat in class.

(c) You must try to avoid making mistakes. (*)

(d) You must stand up when the teacher comes into the room.

(e) You should try to ask questions.(*)

(f) You should ask your teacher if you don't understand something.(*)

(g) You are not allowed to speak to your classmates during the lesson.(*)

(h) You should always ask permission before leaving the classroom.

(i) You should never speak Japanese in class.(*)

(j) You shouldn't speak too loudly in class.(*)

1. Hand out the rules and check understanding.

2. Put the students into groups and give them a time limit to discuss whether they think each one is true or false in their new context.

3. Bring the groups back to a plenary discussion in which you take part, helping to alter their perceptions as and when necessary. Ask *them* to tell you about Japanese classroom rules.

The Japanese educational system trains students to expect binary oppositions; doubt and uncertainty are not valued very highly. One of the main points of this activity is to start to make students aware that there can be an element of negotiation in formulating rules in many classrooms and that they have a contribution to make.

* The asterisked 'rules' are the ones which tend to be different in the writers' classrooms from Japanese classrooms. Japanese learners will not generally be used to the idea of making mistakes and talking loudly in class.

NB: Don't worry if the groups' discussions lapse into Japanese. This is not a language exercise per se, but learner-training. With a group who have just arrived from Japan, you may well decide to let them discuss it in Japanese, at least partly.

Development

An enjoyable follow-up to this activity is for students to write their own rules for the class. This is very effective when it is done as a pyramid discussion (see below for procedure). This is best done a few days or even a week after the initial discussion, once students have got used to the *modus operandi* of your classroom.

Pyramid discussion: procedure

(for a group of twelve)

1. Put students into groups of three and ask them to write their five most important rules for their current class.

2. Put the groups of three together to form two groups of six. Ask them to put their

Safety and Challenge

ten rules together and to decide on the five most important.

3. Put the groups together to come back as a plenary group of twelve. Again, the group reduces the ten rules to five.

4. Students dictate their rules to you. Write them on a large sheet of paper on the classroom wall. You can all then refer to them whenever there's a need. It is also a good idea to incorporate the rules into a weekly assessment meeting so that the rules become a living reality for the class.

Phrase-gathering

Rationale

Phrase-gathering is intended to train students to learn how to 'gather' language from everywhere and anywhere. This is intended to move students away from the idea that you can only acquire language in the classroom, an idea which is certainly not confined to Japanese students. We use the metaphor of hunter-gathering for this type of activity. In this particular example, students are given a licence to take language from each other in a way which is quite counter-cultural.

Activity

Class type: monolingual or multilingual

Level: any

Materials needed: each student should have a piece of writing they have had marked. This should not be heavily corrected, since students might well feel ashamed of showing it to the others. They should each carry paper and pencil.

Preparation: arrange the furniture so that people can move around

Safety/challenge: (●)

Time: 45-60 minutes

Skills: reading, vocabulary extension

Procedure

1. Ask students to display their piece of writing on the desk in front of them. Tell them they should read all the texts and note down any words or phrases that they think could be useful to know and that they themselves would not have thought of using. They should call for help either from you or from the person who wrote it if they are not clear about the meaning or how it could be used in other contexts.

2. Elicit some chosen phrases or vocabulary onto the board, at least one from each student and go through them quickly.

3. Ask the students to form two, three or four teams, each of which should send a representative to the front of the class. There they should stand facing their team with their back turned to the board so that they cannot see it.

4. Explain the rules of this team competition. When you point to an item they should give their representative information to enable them to say it to you. They mustn't use spelling, or say or mouth it, but anything else is fine. They can use gesture, say it in other words, 'sounds like'... etc. (You may want to allow the use of Japanese particularly with a low level class.)

5. When their representative has it right they should put up their hand to attract your attention and say it. The first representative to say it correctly, gets the point for their team. It's a good idea for you to stand where you can see the representatives' faces after pointing to an item, or to have an assistant referee.

6. Play the game until you have used all the items on the board and any other recent vocabulary you want to recycle. When the game is over you could finish by helping students to make flashcards for use in other lessons. They should have either the Japanese translation or the phonemic transcription on the back.

Development

See 'Fishing in the Stream' and 'Reversee' in *More Grammar Games* by Davis and Rinvolucri. See also *Wordcloud* page 12 for another extension.

There is a natural progression from 'gathering' language in the classroom itself, to hunter-gathering for language in other classrooms and, eventually, in the outside world. Examples of such activities are: using recording machines in the street, in cafés and shops, then coming back to the classroom and transcribing tapes.

Cacophony

Rationale

The idea behind *Cacophony* is to start students asking questions and receiving answers. This is a reframing of the classroom and one which is very counter-cultural. Therefore it can only be done playfully and lightly.

The standing or hopping on one leg provides a fun motivation for getting your question answered! It is very 'risky' and only to be used when you know your students well and have built up a lot of safety. Not to be used on the first day!

Activity

Class type: monolingual or multilingual

Level: lower intermediate-advanced

Materials needed: none

Preparation: none

Safety/challenge: ⬤

Time: 30 minutes

Skills: speaking, asking questions

Procedure

1. *Warmer:* ask everyone to think of sounds they can make with their mouths. Give them time to experiment. Go round the class in turn so that everyone can demonstrate their chosen sound. They should all be different. Everyone makes their sounds at the same time (loudly). The warmer is designed to raise energy levels and to give the students permission to make a lot of noise.

2. Now ask students to imagine they are asked to speak for one minute on any topic of their choice: someone they know well or something that they saw... anything at all. Give them time for silent rehearsal with their eyes closed.

3. Ask for a volunteer to speak to the class for one minute on their chosen topic. Tell students that after listening to this they will each ask just one question.

4. Once the student has started speaking, it is a game in which the 'questioners' compete for the speaker's attention in order to have their questions answered. They should stand (or hop) on one leg until they have been answered and then they should sit down. The last one to remain standing up is the loser.

5. Play the game several times with different speakers. This activity is a good follow-on from *Photofantasies*. The one-minute speaking topic then becomes the true version of each person's photo.

Development

In order to get their questions answered, students have to find ways of attracting the attention of the speaker. This will inevitably bring up issues of turn-taking, overlap, eye contact and raising eyebrows.

This game gives a good opportunity to talk about the strategies that students use and their effectiveness, and for the teacher to suggest alternatives.

Safety and Challenge

Oops! I Got it Right!

Rationale

One of the main features of language-learning in Japan is the focus on eradication of mistakes. This insistence on accuracy understandably gives Japanese learners a very low tolerance for error and it makes them very tense! In the context of our classrooms, they have to 're-learn' how to make mistakes or at least be much more tolerant of them. This activity turns the idea of getting rid of mistakes upside down: students are encouraged to put mistakes back into their work. This is so counter-cultural that you'll get lots of laughing, the students will become much less tense and they'll become much less frightened of mistakes!

Activity

Class type: monolingual (but easily adapted for use in mixed classes)

Level: intermediate

Materials needed: a list of typical Japanese errors. You may use our list but it is better for students to collect these errors over a period of time (on a wallposter) from their work. You might like to have an errors monitor for each day, or do it with the whole class at the end of each day/week. You will also need a sheet of corrected sentences taken from student texts.

Preparation: write out the list of errors below

Safety/challenge: (●)

Time: 45-60 minutes

Skills: reading, writing, sensitisation to errors

Procedure

1. Put the list of errors out of sight and ask students to see how many they can remember. Give them five to ten minutes.

2. Refer students to the list of typical errors to see which ones they forgot. Answer any queries.

3. Give out the sheet of correct sentences. Tell students that these sentences were taken from their writing and originally contained typical Japanese mistakes. Ask them to edit each sentence so that it again contains a typical error. They should aim to have re-introduced all of the typical errors by the end of the sheet. Take in the sheets for marking

Some typical Japanese errors

- omission of articles
- missing plurals
- missing third person 's'
- missing/wrong pronouns e.g. he/she confusion
- adjective/noun confusion e.g. I feel happiness
- overuse of possessive e.g. last night's party's meal

Development

A great way to reuse this activity is to collect stories from individual students and write them up for them, corrected. These should be personal stories, relating to the students' lives and told orally. Students then present their story to the group through your text. Later you can ask them to reintroduce as many typical errors as they can into your text. We first learned this idea of writing up students' oral stories from Mario Rinvolucri. It works very well indeed with Japanese learners, who enjoy presenting their stories to the others in correct and natural English. It makes use of one of the strengths of the Japanese – their ability to work.

Section C

Developing Discussion Skills

Introduction

Japanese learners often find it easier to write than to speak in class, a fact which stems from their previous educational experience. Generally speaking, in classes in Japan contribution from learners is low, even in a language learning class. This is partly due to very large classes and partly due to the traditional idea of the importance of the *sensei* (teacher) and the student's duty to receive knowledge.

Spontaneous speaking or discussion, of the type encouraged in many language-learning classrooms, does not come easily to most Japanese students.

Silent Discussion

Rationale

The debate style of discussion with vigorous taking of positions prevalent in the West is foreign to the Japanese tradition. Giving personal opinions does not have the value we accord it in our culture. This activity is therefore good cross-cultural training and could form part of an induction programme.

Silent Discussion allows Japanese learners to have a discussion in the mode that is most comfortable for them. This has the effect of letting them practise putting forward opinions in a safe context. Over-challenging aspects, such as the need for speed and spontaneity, are taken away. Individual students are not put on the spot; they cannot 'lose face'. Japanese people also tend to be much more comfortable with silence than we are in the West.

In the multilingual classroom, this activity 'opens up' the Japanese to the non-Japanese, helping them to see that, though Japanese students do not say everything they think, they are considering the issues. *Silent Discussion* has an interesting effect on class dynamics; during a silent writing activity of this type, different individuals come to the fore. The dynamic is quite different from a speaking class. This will gradually have an effect on other types of class as students become aware of the deeper dynamic.

The quality of thinking when we have to *write* our opinions is markedly more profound. This makes the activity good training for students of all nationalities.

Safety and Challenge

Activity

Class type: monolingual or multilingual

Level: elementary-advanced, low-risk

Materials needed: lots of sheets of paper, pens (large coloured pens if you want to do wall work later)

Preparation: minimal

Safety/challenge: (•)

Time: 30-45 minutes

Skills: reading, writing

Procedure

1. Ask students to sit on the floor, or if possible around a boardroom style table. This activity works best if students are close to each other, but not too close, since you want to avoid the feeling that students have to join in the whole time.

2. Sit as part of the group with the sheets of paper in front of you. Silently, start writing statements at the top of the sheets. It is best if they can be provocative statements on the same theme, perhaps following on from a class activity such as watching a video together, reading a story or an article.

3. As you write, push the sheets out, silently inviting the students to add their own comments whenever they wish. The idea is to get a number of 'strands' going so that after some time, there are a number of discussions taking place, loosely around the same theme. Do not worry if some students do not become involved immediately, or indeed at all. It is much safer than a speaking activity and students almost always take part eventually. The discussion will go through slow periods and periods of intense activity. Some students will participate a lot, others not so much.

4. Allow everyone to read all the discussions. There is no need for oral feedback, though you will find that students will refer to the discussion in follow-up classes. Don't correct overtly at first. As the students gain in confidence, you can start subtly introducing useful discursive language.

You can also use it as a pre-task for an activity, to get the students thinking about the issues. An example of this would be on the theme of education, where the lead statements or questions are:

> 'Discipline is the most important aspect of a school.'

> 'Children should study only what they enjoy.'

> 'Did you enjoy school ?' Why/why not ? (*)

> 'The purpose of life is to be happy.'
> (A. S. Neill)

> 'School should prepare us for life.'

Always put a question like(*) in. Some people find it easier to discuss education from their personal experience. It is good to have a choice.

We have used the silent discussions from these statements as a lead-in to the whole class watching a video about Summerhill, the experimental school in Suffolk.

They could equally well be used as a lead-in to reading, either about Summerhill or some other educational issue from a magazine or newspaper. However, silent discussion lends itself to all kinds of topics (see Development).

As you go through the course, move gradually towards personal opinions. Try at first to choose something that every student could say something about.

Development

This is a very adaptable activity with a potentially large number of spin-offs. You can choose one topic or several, perhaps all linked to a similar theme. The task of providing lead statements can be delegated to a few, or all of the students. Following a group reading or video-viewing, each student can be invited to write one comment which is then used the next day as a lead statement.

Why not:

- use it as a warmer for a larger (oral) discussion, with two or three silent discussions going on? The groups then come together well prepared for the oral part.

- use it to discuss a class reader?
- use it as a quiet feedback time at the end of the day?
- stick the final discussion on the walls for a reading and correction slot?
- have it as a regular session, led by a different student each time, on a theme that he or she finds interesting?
- use it to subtly 'input language' in a context where students are fully engaged ? (You can contribute to the discussion once it's really got going and they're interested.)

Why?

Rationale

One of the features of discursive speaking within the western tradition is the ability to say why one holds a certain opinion or believes a certain thing. This can be quite difficult for Japanese people, partly because, since modesty is so highly valued, no-one really wants to set him/herself up as an expert. There is also the *hito ni warawaremasu* or 'people will laugh at you' fear that comes from teacher and peer pressure within the Japanese system.

The idea behind this activity is to help Japanese learners practise arguments in a safe context before taking part in the discussion with non-Japanese. The topic is also something they are familiar with, indeed they are experts in Japanese customs and habits.

The idea of pairing Japanese students up to prepare arguments in advance is, incidentally, a good way of training Japanese learners for all kinds of discussions.

Note that there will be a strong tendency for the Japanese group to try to achieve consensus in their initial discussion. At first you should not be too worried about this, though you may want to lead them gently towards conclusions which are individual,

rather than either true or false. For example, with statement (f). Eating sweet things is less common in Japan than in the West, though some families may well eat a lot of sweet things – there will be individual differences.

Activity

Class type: monolingual, in preparation for joining up with a non-Japanese, or multilingual class which you split Japanese/non-Japanese

Level: elementary-advanced

Materials needed: true/false discussion sheet (see below)

Preparation: true/false sheet

Safety/challenge:

Time: 45 minutes

Skills: reading, speaking

Procedure

1. Pair up the students and give them a true/false sheet.

2. Instruct students to say whether each statement is generally true or generally false. Tell them that later on they will have to explain their reasons to a group of non-Japanese, so that they should ask each other why/why not each statement is true or false.

3. Go round listening in, asking them why when they are not pushing each other enough.

True or False ?

(a) Japanese houses tend to be very large and spacious.

(b) Japanese people never wash in the bath.

(c) If you are given a present by a Japanese person you immediately open it and show delight.

(d) Japanese people usually eat their main meal at lunchtime.

(e) Japanese people are very sensitive to people showing anger.

(f) Eating sweet things is not common in Japan.

Safety and Challenge

(g) Japanese people don't usually socialise at home.

(h) Japanese people often smile or laugh when embarrassed or confused.

(i) All Japanese people can use chopsticks well.

(j) Members of a Japanese family usually eat together.

Development

The follow-on from this discussion is to put Japanese with non-Japanese, in groups of four or five. The non-Japanese have had their own discussion around the true/false sheet and tried to predict answers when they are not sure. The aim is for the non-Japanese to find out as much as they can in a short time. It's a good idea to give a time limit, though you may decide not to keep strictly to time if the discussion is going well.

You can switch things round the next time, with the Japanese students trying to find out about the others.

Six Thinking Hats

Rationale

The idea for this activity is taken from Edward de Bono's *Six Hat Thinking*. The basic premise is that human beings think in different ways for different purposes (see below). Problems sometimes occur when we try to mix up types of thinking. De Bono uses the idea of different coloured hats to represent different types of thinking.

To put it simply, Japanese students often seem to confine themselves to 'white hat thinking' in contexts where westerners might also be allowed to use 'red hat' and 'green hat' thinking. A good discussion in western terms would include all hats. We must stress here that we are talking about context and appropriacy. Culturally, it seems that we have different ideas about the types of thinking required in different situations.

Activity

Class type: monolingual or multilingual

Level: intermediate

Materials: six paper hats coloured black, yellow, green, red, white, and blue

Preparation: make or ask students to make six paper hats and colour them

Safety/challenge: ●

Time: 45-60 minutes

Skills: discussion

Procedure

1. Write the six colours on the board and elicit the associated feelings. For example, red may signify anger, danger, passion etc.

2. Ask students to match the six colours to the list below. The best way is to have a set of cards with the definitions written on them.

Ways of Thinking	(correct matchings)
White	Facts, figures, information
Blue	Cool, detached, thinking about thinking
Yellow	Optimistic
Green	Creative, fertile, new ideas
Black	Negative, pessimistic
Red	Emotions, feelings, intuition

3. Six friends are discussing whether to throw a party at their flat. Can you say what colour the following comments are?

It would cost the same as last time. *(white)*

We have two weeks to prepare if we start tomorrow. *(white)*

We could make it a fancy dress party this year! *(green)*

Why don't we make it a theme party? *(green)*

I don't think anyone would come so near Christmas. They'll all be with their families. Even if they did come, the neighbours would probably complain about the noise. *(black)*

Oh, I expect lots of people would come. It would be wonderful. *(yellow)*

We can invite the neighbours too. *(yellow)*

We really need to decide today. *(blue)*

Shall we take a vote on it this afternoon? *(blue)*

I'm dying to see Sue and Ted and everyone. *(red)*

Oh, I do hope we can do it! *(red)*

4. Ask students to get into six groups or pairs, depending on numbers. Hand out the hats, one to each pair and tell them to think of comments on the following suggestions.

(a) *Teacher:* Shall we watch a video in class tomorrow?

(b) *Teacher:* How about a trip to the country at the weekend ?

They need only display the colour, not put the hats on. They should only make comments in keeping with their hat.

5. Have plenary feedback.

Development

You can come back to this 'frame' for future discussions or analysing recorded discussions/dialogues.

Aizuchi Awareness

Rationale

One of the difficult things about learning a foreign language is acquiring the nonverbal and paralinguistic features that accompany speech. When speaking to each other Japanese people often use sounds and phrases such as *ne, ha, so desu-ka, honto ni*, to show the speaker that they are listening to what is being said. These sounds help establish communication between speaker and listener and are called *aizuchi*, which literally means 'chiming in'. They function rather like sounds and phrases like 'mmm' 'really' and 'I see' in English, except that *aizuchi* are used even more frequently.

Since *aizuchi* are so important in Japanese as 'encouragers', learners are keen to know how to do the same thing in English. This activity helps to heighten the student's awareness of *aizuchi* in English and to enable the student to start using them for themselves. A possible danger is that students may be tempted to learn them as formulae. Students should be encouraged to develop a feel for them.

As important as the verbal 'encouragers', are the paralinguistic ones. As a teacher, it is useful to train yourself to closely observe what these are. Eye contact is very important, as is the raising of the eyebrows. Both are something that westerners do, but Japanese people do not. In fact, constant eye contact is seen as very aggressive.

Activity

Class type: monolingual

Level: elementary-intermediate

Materials needed: none

Preparation: minimal

Safety/challenge: ◉

Time: 30 minutes

Skills: speaking

Procedure

1. Introduce the topic of *aizuchi* and get the students to tell you some of the ways that Japanese people show that they are listening, both verbal and non-verbal.

2. Pair students up and instruct them to have a conversation in Japanese, but without the use of *aizuchi*.

3. Ask them for feedback.

This will help to raise awareness of the importance of *aizuchi* and to help them to understand how westerners might feel without the right 'encouragers'.

Safety and Challenge

Development

As a later follow-on, record a short conversation between yourself and a friend or colleague. The conversation should be as natural as possible, so choose a 'real' topic, one that is really of interest to both of you. You can sometimes find good recorded tapes, but these homemade ones are often the best.

Transcribe the conversation, but leave gaps for the 'oh reallys' etc. Start the class with a brainstorm of English *aizuchi*. The length of this discussion will depend on how long the students have been in an English-speaking environment.

Give the students the transcription before listening. They read the transcription and check understanding. They then work in pairs to put in suitable noises, words and phrases. Then play the tape and the students correct their versions. Follow up with a discussion of different possibilities.

A nice follow-on is for the students to 'practise' your conversation with the *aizuchi*. Then they can move on to their own conversations and try out the words and phrases. A good homework activity is for the student to choose a 'new' English *aizuchi* and try to use it in a real conversation, for example with their host mother or father.

This is not just a one-off activity. You can carry on practising throughout the course.

Getting a Comment in

Rationale

This is a possible follow-up to *Aizuchi Awareness*, though it also stands on its own. The aim is to sensitise students to the need to keep a discussion/conversation going by the interjection of appropriate comments.

The final role-play should be great fun, with students competing to get their comments in first.

Activity

Class type: monolingual or multilingual

Level: intermediate and above

Materials/ equipment needed: short, discursive text, a tape of someone giving their opinion orally

Preparation: see below

Safety/challenge: ◉

Time: two hours, over two to three lessons

Skills: speaking

Procedure

1. Ask a 'monitor' to make a note of your comments during an activity like *Good and New* (see Section E). They will be comments such as 'that's interesting', 'oh, really', 'did you?' etc.

2. Ask the student/students to report back to the whole class. Make up a list of comments.

3. Give the students a copy of a short discursive text, perhaps someone expressing their opinion. It is best to use one that students have already seen. Ask the students to 'interact with the text' by inserting comments at appropriate places.

4. Check and discuss with the whole class.

5. Do the same with someone giving their opinion orally. Work with the tape and a transcript. (You can even get the students to transcribe it).

6. Two students take part in a role play of a longish conversation that they've already practised in another context. All the other students have slips of paper with a comment on, one comment each. They must add their comments into the conversation appropriately.

Development

You can make this activity more and more challenging as the students gain in confidence. One way of injecting urgency is to talk to the students on a topic they haven't heard before and ask them to interject comments orally.

Section D Cultural Surf-riding

Introduction

This section contains generally high-challenge activities. The challenge comes mainly from the fact that they ask students to behave in a way which is counter-cultural, certainly within the context of the classroom.

An important aspect of our approach to teaching Japanese students is that we believe it is sometimes a good idea to talk explicitly about cultural differences. Information is useful. So, in the same way that it is helpful for us as teachers to know certain cultural facts about Japan, it is useful for our students to have information about western culture.

This is not to say that information will bring about immediate changes in behaviour – nor that it should. We see it as the first step in understanding and in allowing students to make choices about how they communicate and behave in the target culture.

What Do You Really Think ?

Rationale

Traditional Japanese concern with interpersonal harmony (*wa*) led to the development of a system of behaviour that includes careful control of facial expressions and body movements. Alongside this, is a highly stylised form of indirect, 'vague' speech designed to avoid commitment or conflict of any kind.

The Japanese, then, deal in two different worlds: *honne*, their true thoughts and intentions and *tatemae*, a kind of screen of superficial statements or utterances created to maintain harmony.

In the West people are also interested in creating harmony, though we tend to approach it in a different way. Within our tradition, it is felt that harmony can best be achieved by being open and honest and working through conflict.

For the Japanese to say what they really think in a normal social context is extremely counter-cultural. It is seen as childish and selfish. In our culture, not to say what you think in certain contexts can be seen as evasive, even devious. Context, however, is very important. All cultures have a certain level of *tatemae*, as part of their politeness. We just have different ways of expressing it.

(You can use the above text for the students' information sheet.)

Japanese students will become sensitised to the differences over a period of time if they stay in an English-speaking environment for long enough. There are some things we can

Safety and Challenge

do in the classroom, though. This is a sensitisation exercise which you can use as a first broaching of the subject. It's also good as part of an induction course before going abroad, or before joining a multinational group if they are already outside Japan.

We believe that there are times when it is appropriate to give the students information about cultural differences. This helps their acculturation and seems to reassure them that their experience is 'normal'.

Activity

Class type: monolingual

Level: intermediate

Materials needed: information sheet

Preparation: none, unless you prepare your own information sheet

Safety/challenge: ◉

Time: 60 minutes

Skills: reading, discussion

Procedure

1. Tell the students that you are going to discuss some differences between the two cultures. Have a short brainstorm of some differences they've found so far.

2. Put the words *wa*, *honne* and *tatemae* on the board. Let the students confer for a few minutes and then see if they can explain the words to you. They might find this difficult, but they should try.

3. Pre-teach words like *conflict , counter-cultural, vague, tradition*. Give out the information sheet.(Use the rationale given for this exercise.) Let them read it and check understanding.

4. The groups then have about 30 minutes to discuss the information and come up with examples from their own experience.

5. Have a discussion in plenary based on their group discussions.

The aim of this sensitisation activity is to provide a safe context in which students can talk about differences which are bound to cause them culture shock. It should be relaxed and low-key.

Development

Once you have opened up the channel to talk about the cultural differences, allow some time in class for talking about them on a regular basis.

Interrupting Game

Rationale

One of the things that Japanese students find very difficult about language classes – and perhaps general interaction in the West – is that people interrupt each other constantly. Generally speaking, there is far more overlap in discourse, especially in what the Japanese regard as the rather formal setting of the classroom.

In multinational groups, Japanese learners often find it hard to survive in what can be the rather discursive, boisterous atmosphere of our classrooms. The focus is on 'communication' and for good or for ill, we often place a high value on speaking.

It is important to acknowledge that there are different modes of communication operating. Neither is good or bad in itself, simply more effective in different situations. We may feel that we do not want to 'change people's behaviour'. However, Japanese students often do suffer greatly because their way of interacting can make them 'invisible' in a mixed nationality group.

We use this activity as part of learner-training and induction for Japanese students who are about to join a multinational group. Of course, if they are in an English-speaking environment long enough, they may well learn to do this naturally, in order to survive. This activity is intended to help to speed the process up. It turns the whole thing into a game and keeps it light.

Activity

Class type: best in a monolingual class

Level: any level

Materials needed: none

Preparation time: none

Safety/challenge: ◉

Time: 20 minutes or more *

Skills: speaking, listening

Procedure

1. Invite a student to speak continuously on a given topic. Initially at least, this should be something fairly easy to talk about, for example 'my family'.

2. Before the student starts speaking, the other students decide on a 'trigger word'. For the first time you may help them to choose a common word e.g. *because* or *maybe*.

3. The other students can interrupt the speaker with a statement, whenever they hear him or her use that word. The student speaking has to quickly work out which word it is and to avoid it, if he or she wants to speak uninterrupted.

Once the speaker has worked out which word it is, it becomes rather like the radio quiz game 'Just a Minute'. The speaker has to get to the end smoothly without repeating the trigger word or phrase.

Good topics for this activity are personal experiences the student may have had. It works best when the student really wants to tell his or her story.

Development

* You can use this activity as a warmer for the first 10 minutes of the class to raise the energy level. Put the class into groups of three or four so that everyone is active.

A nice variation on this is 'Interrupting with Questions'. The student tells a story, perhaps an incident which happened to him

or her, or on a theme e.g. 'an accident I had'. The story should either be personal or well-known by the speaker. The speaker sets off telling his or her story. The others try to stop the speaker reaching the end of the story by asking questions. Each question must be answered before the speaker can go on. Once the speaker has reached the end, someone else tells another story.

Taking Over

Rationale

This activity is designed to train students to take the initiative in the classroom situation. This would be good for an induction course for students joining a multilingual class. The idea is to start on a physical level and move into the linguistic.

We always accompany this type of training with 'straightforward telling' the students about the differences between educational cultures (see for example *What Do You Really Think ?* p.29)

Activity

Class type: monolingual or multilingual

Level: any

Materials needed: none

Preparation: none

Safety/challenge: ◉

Time: 20 minutes

Skills: speaking, vocabulary

Procedure

1. Tell the students to stand in a circle.

2. Start off with three instructions which the students are familiar with e.g. ' Hiroko, go and touch something blue'. The students do as you say. Then elicit more instructions from the group, with students performing each instruction, until you say: 'Somebody take over'.

3. A student then takes over and gives three instructions of a different set e.g. 'Sit

down, stand up, touch your toes', elicits more from the other students, and then asks someone else to take over.

4. Somebody has to take over immediately! The idea is to keep going until everyone has had a turn at taking over.

Development

This is a great activity for the revision of vocabulary or structure. Once the students have practised the 'physical' instructions, you can move on to lexical sets, e.g. fruit ('Pass me the orange') furniture ('Sit on the chair') geographical features ('Point to the mountain on the map').

Once the students have got the hang of it, you could start off with a quick vocabulary/ structure review of the week's lessons – just what has been covered rather than details – so that students are prepared for what is to follow.

Oi !

Rationale

The main idea behind this activity is to get learners used to reading faster, though it has other spin-offs. The tendency for Japanese learners is to read slowly and try to understand every single word. This forces them along and makes it fun too!

One of the spin-offs is that it gets learners shouting out and contradicting the teacher.

Activity

Class type: monolingual or multilingual

Level: any

Materials needed: short reading text

Preparation: minimal

Safety/challenge:

Time: 10 minutes

Skills: reading, listening

Procedure

1. Choose a short text which the students will be able to understand without too many problems.

2. Tell them that you're going to give them the text, that it's easy, but that they don't need to think about meaning for the moment.

3. Start reading the text at normal speed, but change some of the words. The students follow your reading and shout Oi! whenever you change a word. If you change the words to something funny, it causes great hilarity. Encourage the students to shout out.

Development

This is a fun introductory activity for any reading skills lesson. It provides the students with an introduction to the text, but doesn't let them get 'bogged down' in it.

A variation on this activity is to dictate a short text to the students. In the final reading-through, change some of the words. Again, encourage the students to shout out and contradict you.

Mime Stories

Rationale

This activity calls for students to do something individually in front of the class. That can be extremely frightening, so the focus is on keeping it light and fun. It helps, though, that students mime rather than speak when they are 'on the spot'. Also, you do it first !

Activity

Class type: monolingual or multilingual

Level: any

Materials: none

Preparation: think of an amusing anecdote and how it could be told in mime

Safety/challenge:

Time: 45-60 minutes

Procedure

1. Ask students to think about funny or embarrassing situations they have been in.

2. Tell them you are going to tell them one of yours in mime.

3. Arrange the furniture so that there is a 'stage' area.

4. Mime a short story or amusing anecdote.

5. Mime it again, but this time elicit what is happening from the students. Shake your head when they guess wrongly and nod when they are right, before continuing the mime.

6. Put them in groups to discuss what they think the mime showed.

7. Tell the story in words. Answer any questions.

8. Ask the students to choose one of their funny situations and look up or ask for the vocabulary they would need to tell it.

9. Students then prepare to mime their story in the same way. They may recruit a helper if they need one.

10. Ask for volunteers to come out and mime their situation.

11. They should mime it a second time while students guess what they are seeing. The performing student should just nod or shake their head.

12. Ask them to tell the story in words and answer any questions as you did. Which did they think was the most amusing story?

Development

Put the students into pairs or groups to prepare a story and tell it to another group who then mime it. This is a nice way of turning this activity into an even more multi-skill one. A way of developing this even further is to ask students to write the story thus turning it into a writing activity.

Letting Go of Tension

Introduction

Though a certain level of tension or stress can be useful in the learning situation, there is a point at which it becomes counterproductive. The classroom, whether in the West or in the East, can be a very stressful environment. Japanese learners have certain expectations of the classroom which can make them 'freeze'. Some of these expectations concern accuracy, correctness and form. Teachers often comment on the fact that outside the classroom, students are much more able to perform than inside. These activities are designed to help students to 'unfreeze'.

Pleasant Memories

Rationale

Pleasant Memories and *Good and New* are activities we have 'borrowed' from the discipline of co-counselling. In co-counselling, we use 'positive frames' to introduce group activities and also to take attention away from negative and distressing events or feelings.

For us, one of the keys to working with Japanese students is finding ways of releasing the tension associated for them with the classroom. We often speak of them 'freezing' in class and therefore the need for 'reframing the classroom'.

You can use *Pleasant Memories* in these situations:

• If the students have been working very hard on an exercise or activity

• If the students have been focused on how difficult something is and they seem stuck.

Activity

1. Sit round in a closed circle with no desks between you. You can do this just on chairs or on the floor.

2. Start off with a pleasant memory of your own. Tell them about it.

3. Invite everyone to talk about a pleasant memory. Gently insist that everyone takes part, even if they can't remember a pleasant memory at first!

4. Keep going until you feel everyone relax. You may offer prompts like: pleasant memories of a beach/the countryside/the sun/flowers/a family occasion/a birthday.

Safety and Challenge

Good and New

Activity

This is a good start to the day. It bridges the gap between what is happening in real life and the life of the group in the classroom. It is a strong 'reframe' of the classroom into a place where students can talk about personal experience.

Class type: monolingual or multilingual

Level: any

Materials needed: none

Preparation: none

Safety/challenge: (•)

Time: 15 minutes

Skills: listening and speaking

1. Sit round in a closed circle.

2. Start off with the question: 'What's good and new?'

3. Students and you yourself take turns to say what's good and new since the last time you met. Examples might be, 'I received a letter from my friend,' 'The sun is shining' or 'I did my homework'. If you find that they can't start, you start. It's important, though, that what they say is true.

Pic Chop Call

Rationale

In this activity we use the visual mode (pictures) and the kinaesthetic mode (moving around the classroom) to relax the students. However, there is a lot of language work in this lesson.

Activity

Class type: monolingual or multilingual

Level: any

Materials needed: four or more pictures that are detailed and show a number of people doing different things. It is ideal to cut large pictures out of magazines and stick them onto thin card.

Preparation: cut each picture into six strips. Shuffle these well and give out as many pictures as there are students. Blutack the remaining pictures semi-hidden around the room.

Safety and challenge:

Time: 30 minutes

Skills: listening, speaking

Procedure

1. Ask students to circulate, describing but not showing their picture to other students. When they find another student who has a piece of the same picture as they have, they should stay together and search for the missing pieces which might be held by another students, or that are semi-hidden around the room.

2. When they have assembled their complete picture on a desk they will call you over and you allocate a letter to each group that has been formed in this way. There will eventually be teams A, B, C and D, and each picture should be laid intact on a flat surface.

3. Holding your own set of complete pictures, you should then call out a description of something you can see happening in one of the strips. For example, 'I can see a little boy building a sandcastle'.

4. Students have to race to find the strip containing this and bring it to you. You then write in pencil on the back the team letter (e.g. Team A) of the student who found it and it is returned to its position. The team with the most marks wins.

Photofantasies

Rationale

There is a high level of personalisation in this activity. Students bring their own photographs and have a chance to talk about them. The visual element 'takes the heat off', relaxing the students and helping them to practise listening and speaking in an informal but focused way.

Activity

Class type: monolingual or multilingual

Level: lower intermediate

Materials needed: photos that students bring in and some of your own. These should preferably be as varied as possible. Try to avoid graduation photos as they are all very similar.

Preparation: minimal

Safety/challenge: (•)

Time: 45 minutes in class and 30 minutes homework

Skills: listening, speaking, writing

Procedure

1. Spread the photos out on a flat surface, face down. Tell the students you are going to show them how to play the game. Take a photo at random, show it to the class and, pretending it is your photo, tell them who is who, where it was taken and when, what the situation was and about anything that 'happened' just before or after the photo was taken. Make it amusing if you can.

2. Ask the real owner of the photo to stand up and to tell the group the truth.

3. Invite students to each pick up any photo, but not their own, and imagine that this is one of their own photographs. They spend a few minutes preparing their fantasy version.

4. Students take it in turns to present a photo and give them out again. Ask students to photocopy (or you do it for

them if this is more convenient) the one they get and to repeat the activity but not in writing. This might be best done for homework. They should leave a space for the real owner of the photo to add his or her version the following day.

5. The following day/lesson, put all the papers on the table and ask students to find their own photo, read what the fake owner wrote on it and then write the true version in the space allowed. Display all/some of the most amusing on the wall/pinboard.

Four Squares

Rationale

This is another activity in which there is some intense language work going on – in this case vocabulary extension, but using non-linguistic media. In *Four Squares* we use music. The students are also encouraged to move around the room, showing them that the classroom is not just a place where you sit still at your desk.

NB: This activity may be difficult if your classroom is very small or your class is very big, or both.

Activity

Class type: any

Level: any

Materials/equipment needed: music cassette and cassette recorder

Preparation: none

Safety/challenge: (•)

Time: 30 minutes

Skills: speaking, intonation

Procedure

1. Elicit onto the board adjectives describing mood states, e.g. *fed up, happy, frightened, embarrassed, sad.*

2. Ask students to categorise these adjectives into four groups. For example:

Safety and Challenge

fed up, miserable and *sad* might be put together under the heading *unhappy*. There will be some that give rise to discussion. Don't discourage this. Some may feel for example that *fed up* should be put with *cross* and *angry*.

3. With the whole class decide on four generic categories. Mark out the room so that there four different areas. Tell students that each area represents one category. For example, *happy, sad, angry, shy.*

4. Put on some music and ask students to walk around the room freely in any direction until the music stops. When it stops they should greet the other students in the same area of the room as they are with *hello* in the manner of the word. They will need to use exaggerated intonation. You might like to model the four *hello's* for them first.

5. Repeat Step 4 several times and then tell students that next time they are going to say more than *hello*. They should also explain the reason for the feeling. For example a student landing in the *happy* square might explain that they have just passed an important exam/won the national lottery/had a baby. They should maintain their happy manner.

6. Students return to their desks. Ask students to tell the class what they were told and, referring to the original list of adjectives, match them with the situations. For example, if a student says she was greeted in the *happy* square by someone who had just received good news from home you might want to offer her the adjectives *delighted, overjoyed* etc.

7. Allow time for students to make notes from the board.

Tic Toc Tac

Rationale

This activity requires intense concentration and yet has laughter triggers which break the tension. It is therefore a classic example of alternating high challenge with safety.

It heightens student awareness of the rhythms of English and how intonation relates to meaning. It enhances their survival English since the situation behind the dialogue is a familiar one for most language learners.

Activity

Class type: monolingual or multilingual

Level: any

Materials needed: Three or four small familiar objects such as a board pen, glue stick and rubber

Preparation: minimal

Safety/challenge:

Time: 20 minutes

Skills: pronunciation: elision/weak forms, stress, intonation, also practice of articles

Procedure

If possible, have the group arranged in a circle.

1. Hold up one of the objects and hand it to a student (A) saying 'This is a tic'.

2. Elicit or give the question 'What is it?' (with rising intonation in the sense of 'what did you call it?')

3. Answer the question 'It's a tic'. Indicate they should hand it to the next student (B) and rehearse the same dialogue with them. Give lots of support and correction and model the dialogue for them for as long as they need it, until it's sounding good. Make it clear to everyone that this is a nonsense word. And that this is a game designed to help with pronunciation and therefore intelligibility.

A: This is a tic.

B: What is it?

C: It's a tic!

4. When it has been right round the class

once or twice and students are producing it well, introduce the second object in the same way. 'This is a toc' but sending it in the other direction around the group. This generally causes laughter as students struggle to remember which is the tic and which is the toc as well as the correct intonation for the dialogue.

5. Introduce the third object as a tac and treat it in the same way. There should now be three objects being passed around and some confusion and laughter as two objects arrive at the same student from different directions.

6. Finally introduce a fourth object. 'This is a tuc'. Since Japanese has a vowel sound which is halfway between 'a' and 'u' this is difficult for them to distinguish. The drill usually collapses in confusion and giggles at this point.

7. Put the dialogue on the board and mark the sentence stresses and the minimal pair (a and u). Use phonemic symbols and pictures.

8. Tell the students you are going to help them distinguish between the sounds. You are going to mouth the word *hut* or *hat* and they should watch carefully to see which you are saying. If they think you are saying *hat* they should point to the right and if they think you are saying *hut* they should point to the left.

9. When most people are able to see the difference in the two sounds by watching your face, some might like to take a turn in your place.

10. Tell the students they are going to do the same exercise as before (Tic, toc, tac) but this time the intonation will be different. Repeat the original activity but this time: 'This is a tic/tac/tuc.' 'What is it?' 'It's a tic/tac/toc.' 'What is it?' (and with falling intonation, in the sense of: *What is it being used for?*) 'It's for writing on the board/ sticking paper/erasing paper'. When this is being produced well

you can reintroduce the original intonation from time to time and ask students to listen carefully for the sentence stress and try to give the appropriate response.

11. Recycle this dialogue often informally in class.

Development

You can use this framework any time you want to do a bit of classic language drilling e.g. for practice of a dialogue:

A: He's gone to Paris.

B: When did he go?

A: He went last week.

Section F — Taking the Focus off Language

Introduction

The tension or stress that we talked about in the last section can be alleviated by taking the focus off language from time to time. This does not mean that we are no longer *concerned* with language, simply that sometimes focusing on it too much is counter-productive. We have found that when students are doing something with their hands or their bodies they can produce language in a less self-conscious and 'tight' way. This helps them to take their attention off accuracy and onto communication. You will also notice that there is a lot of emphasis on the visual in this section.

Artcards 'Get to Know'

Rationale

When students are getting to know each other, it's good to have something concrete to talk about. In this case, the postcards provide the motivation for speaking and allow students to talk at a deeper level than they would do normally on first meeting. At the same time it's safe because, although in one sense they are talking about themselves, they can also choose their own depth.

With Japanese students it's important to take their attention away from accuracy and draw it towards communication. Trying to be accurate can often make them tense and lead them to produce stilted language.

Onion circles take away the social embarrassment of choosing partners and ensures that each person speaks to everyone. The music in the background reframes the classroom.

Activity

Class type: monolingual or multilingual

Level: elementary - advanced

Materials/equipment needed: a large selection of postcards (artcards work best, preferably have at least four times as many cards as students), a cassette player and a music cassette

Preparation: none

Safety and challenge: (•)

Time: 30-40 minutes

Skills: speaking

Safety and Challenge

Procedure

1. Spread out the artcards on a large table or on the floor.

2. Invite students to come up and choose three cards that attract them. They should not think too hard about this. Demonstrate by choosing some yourself and telling the class what you like about them. Perhaps they remind you of somewhere, someone, a mood.

3. Students sit in two concentric circles of equal numbers so that each faces a partner i.e. the outer one facing inwards and the inner facing outwards. If space is not available, see alternatives.

4. Play some music and ask the outer circle of students to walk anticlockwise, stopping and sitting down opposite someone in the inner ring only when the music stops.

5. In the pairs they find themselves in, they should each show their cards one at a time, explaining what attracted them to each picture.

6. When they hear the music starting they should say goodbye to their partner, and as before, the outer ring will walk anticlockwise around the inner circle until the music stops, at which point they sit down opposite their next partner and repeat the task.

Encourage students to call you for help if they are stuck for vocabulary.

7. When most people have spoken to each other the activity ends.

8. In plenary ask:

(a) if anyone has learned something new about any of their classmates

(b) if anyone would like to give a new title to any of the cards they chose before returning them.

Then take the cards back in.

Development

1. This activity can also be done using a collection of small objects.

2. If space is tight then instead of concentric circles you could use two rows of chairs back-to-back or do it as a 'cocktail': people walking freely around the room finding new partners every time the music stops.

Retitling Artcards

Rationale

This is another activity which makes use of the type of postcards of paintings mentioned above, though the activity works best if they are new to the students. This time they are a springboard for writing, which *can* cause tension. In this case the writing is a free expression of feeling and should not be a strain. The focus is on the feeling, not the language, and you should not be tempted to correct.

We find that Japanese people are often very visual and enjoy talking about paintings. We also find that it is very important, and not only with Japanese students, to decorate the walls of the classroom if at all possible.

Activity

Class type: monolingual or multilingual

Level: any

Materials/equipment needed: a large selection of postcards of paintings (see above) sheets of paper, music is optional

Preparation: lay out the sheets of paper on the desks.

Safety and challenge: (•)

Time: 30-40 minutes

Skills: speaking, writing

Procedure

1. Choose a number of postcards and place each one on one sheet of paper. Use a number of different desks so that they are

spread around the room and the students can walk around comfortably. There should be at least as many cards as there are students, preferably more, and of different styles.

2. Instruct the students to walk around the room looking at the postcards and to write a title when they feel like it. They should write their title at the bottom of the paper, then fold it under so that the next student cannot see their title and be influenced by it. Give them plenty of time to walk around and think.

3. When the students have finished, unfold the paper and let them look at all the different titles. Is there a title they really like, apart from their own? Discussion will naturally follow.

4. Ask the students to choose one of the paintings they particularly like, to return to their seats and to write a short piece about why they like it.

5. Stick the postcards, the titles and the pieces of writing on poster paper around the room.

Musical Daydream

Rationale

This is a relaxing activity which works on the principle of moving from images through to language. This, as we have seen before, seems a particularly effective route for Japanese learners.

Activity

Class type: monolingual or multilingual

Level: any

Materials/equipment needed: two pieces of taped instrumental music* and a cassette player

Preparation: just choosing the music

Safety/challenge: (•)

Time: 30 minutes

Skills: speaking

Procedure

1. Have music playing quietly. Invite students to spend a few minutes with their heads down listening to the music. They should notice the pictures that come into their minds, if any.

2. When the music is finished ask them to work in pairs and describe their internal images.

3. Repeat the exercise with a different piece of music. Students should try to see the pictures described to them by their classmates. They should feel free to elaborate and edit them and make them their own.

*Choose a piece of music you particularly like. We have used a variety of pieces from Kate Bush and Pat Metheny through to Mozart.

Development

An interesting development from this activity is for the students to listen to music while looking at pictures of people; postcards from a portrait gallery such as The National Portrait Gallery are good for this (cover up the names on the back!).

Again, let the students relax while listening, but ask the students if they have any feelings about the personality of the person they're looking at. This is a good way of introducing vocabulary to describe personality. You can move into stories, scenes, background, almost anywhere from here. The combination of the music and the pictures is very suggestive.

Safety and Challenge

Frozen Cameos

Rationale

Frozen Cameos is a way of giving feedback on readers/stories which the students have been reading. It's ideal if students have been reading different readers so that there's an information gap. However, you can use it if they've been reading the same reader to talk about favourite scenes.

The rationale behind it is to use a visual means of accessing a written text.

Activity

Class type: monolingual or multilingual

Levels: any

Materials needed: class readers

Preparation: students have been reading different readers

Safety/challenge: (•)

Time: 45 minutes

Skills: speaking, listening

Procedure

Part A: (groups)

1. Put students in small groups of three or four. Tell them they have, say, 20 minutes for the first part.

2. Each student chooses a scene from the reader they have been reading.

3. One student describes the scene visually to the members of his or her group and uses a combination of physically moving the other students and verbal instructions to get them into position. The scene may include all of the group or only one or two.

4. Each student does the same, so that the group has produced three or four 'frozen cameos' – rather like a video when you pause it. There is no speaking in the scene, just a 'picture'.

Part B: (the whole class)

The groups perform the 'frozen cameos' for the other groups. Students from the other groups ask questions about the scene and the student who has read that book answers.

Development

Once the students are used to 'freezing' scenes like this, you can use it for all kinds of language work.

Some ideas:

• put students into a frozen cameo to elicit a scene for a dialogue

• use frozen cameo as a human picture dictation.

Booklist

There are hundreds of books on Japan. Here is a selection of books that we have found useful as an introduction to Japanese life and culture:

General

Pictures from the Water Trade by John David Morley (published by Flamingo). This is an excellent insight into Japan by a *gaijin* (foreigner).

The Roads to Sata by Alan Booth (published by Penguin). Alan Booth walked all the way through Japan and wrote about his experiences.

The *Japan in Your Pocket* series (published by JTB.)

Japanese Language

The BBC course: *Japanese Language and People*, books, videos and cassettes. A good basic speaking and listening course.

Basic Japanese Grammar by Everett F. Bleier (published by Tuttle.)

Japanese Women

Womansword by Kitteredge Cherry (published by Kodansha). What Japanese words betray about attitudes to women.

Fiction

Haiku by Bashō. The Japanese created this lyrical form, short poems of great intensity, and Bashō was the greatest exponent.

Beauty and Sadness by Yasunari Kawabata (published by Penguin). A novel which gives you a very good idea of the sparse lyricism of much of Japanese literature.

Kitchen by Banana Yoshimoto written in the early 90s. This first novel by a young Japanese woman created quite a stir when it first came out.

Journal

The Japanese Learner edited by Katie Gray:
Department for Continuing Education
University of Oxford
1, Wellington Square
Oxford~
OX1 2JA

DELTA Publishing aims to provide teachers of English - wherever they are and whatever their teaching situation - with innovative, creative, practical resource material to help them in their everyday teaching tasks.

For further information and a copy of the DELTA Publishing catalogue, please contact Eileen Fryer:

DELTA Publishing
39 Alexandra Road
Addlestone
Surrey KT15 2PQ
England

Tel: +44 (0) 1932 854776

Fax: +44 (0) 1932 849528

Email:delta@deltabooks.co.uk

Creative materials for creative teachers

ENGLISH TEACHING *professional*

ENGLISH TEACHING *professional* is an independent, quarterly magazine offering teachers of English worldwide a variety of practical, accessible, up-to-date features and articles concerned with classroom solutions and professional development.

For information on how to subscribe to ENGLISH TEACHING *professional*, please contact:

ENGLISH TEACHING *professional*
The Swan Business Centre
Fishers Lane
Chiswick
London W4 1RX
England

Tel: +44 (0) 181 896 0893

Fax: +44 (0) 181 896 0894

Email:etpemail@aol.com

If teaching English is your profession,
ENGLISH TEACHING *professional is your magazine*